ANIMAL CHAMPIONS 2

Published by Creative Education, 123 South Broad Street, Mankato, Minnesota 56001

Library of Congress Cataloging-in-Publication Data

Shaw, Marjorie B. / Elwood, Ann.
Animal champions 2 / series created by John Bonnett Wexo: written by Marjorie B. Shaw and Ann Elwood: zoological consultant, Charles R. Schroeder: scientific consultant, Charles Radcliffe.
p. cm. — (Zoobooks)
Includes index.
Summary: A look at the amazing feats animals perform as well as a discussion about the wide variety of animals that populate our earth.
ISBN 0-88682-774-4
1. Animals—Miscellanea—Juvenile literature. [1. Animals—Miscellanea.] I. Title. II. Series: Zoo books (Mankato, Minn.)
QL49.W48   1996
591—dc20   91-11775   CIP AC

ANIMAL CHAMPIONS 2

Creative Education

Art Credits

Paintings by Richard Orr

Photographic Credits

Front Cover: Ron Garrison (*Zoological Society of San Diego*)

Page Eight: Upper Right, Ron Garrison (*Zoological Society of San Diego*); **Lower Left,** Anthony Bannister (*NHPA*)

Page Nine: Upper Left, Jen and Des Bartlett (*Bruce Coleman, Inc.*); **Lower Right,** Thomas Mangelsen (*Images of Nature*)

Page Ten: George Glod (*Superstock*)

Page Thirteen: Upper Left, Warren Garst (*Tom Stack & Associates*); **Middle,** Stephen Dalton (*Animals Animals*)

Pages Fourteen and Fifteen: Stephen Dalton (*NHPA*)

Page Sixteen: George D. Dodge and Dale R. Thompson (*Bruce Coleman, Inc.*)

Pages Eighteen and Nineteen: Stephen Dalton (*Photo Researchers*)

Page Twenty-One: E.R. Degginger (*Animals Animals*)

Page Twenty-Three: George Holton (*Photo Researchers*)

Our Thanks To:
G.P. Edwards (*Florida State Collection of Arthropods*); David Faulkner (*San Diego Natural History Museum*); Blaine Hebert (*California State University, Northridge*); Mike Greer and Nancy Pajeau (*Brookfield Zoo*); Andy Kaufman; Mike Brown; Casey and Lizzie Elwood; Joe Selig

Cover Photo: Bearded dragon

Contents

All animals are champions. Their skills are what help them to survive. But some animals regularly perform what, to us, seem like spectacular feats.

It seems that all the animals on these pages are in a great race. But, apart from domestic, trained animals, only humans use their running skill to race. The wild members of the animal kingdom run either to escape a predator, chase down a meal, or to cover vast distances in search of food.

Some animals can run fast for short distances, and some can run medium distances. Others are long-distance champions. And some are so well protected and adapted to their environment that they don't need to run at all!

In this book, you will read about the fastest, biggest, smallest, and strongest animals. Just remember that all these *superlative* animals simply use the skills required for survival in their environments.

Humans usually run for fun, for exercise, and to compete. But the fastest person in the world is a slowpoke compared to many animals. Top speed for a human is just under 27 miles per hour. Although this record will eventually be broken, humans will never reach the speeds of the jackrabbit and the cheetah.

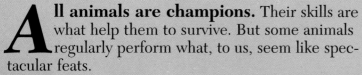

The giant tortoise is one of the slowest-moving animals on earth. Its top speed is less than 1/4 mile per hour. But why should it run? Like all land tortoises, it can pull its head and legs inside its shell. Its best defense is to sit like a rock.

Many predators would like to have jackrabbit for dinner. To avoid being eaten, a jackrabbit must move very fast. By using its powerful leg muscles, it often escapes predators by zigzagging in big jumps at speeds up to 45 miles per hour.

There is nothing faster on two legs than an ostrich. This big flightless bird can run 35 miles per hour over flat grassland. This ability helps to protect it from lions and other predators. Ostriches need to run fast because they can't fly—their wings are too small and their bodies are too heavy.

Wild horses must escape predators and cover long distances to find water and good grazing. To meet these needs, they are built for endurance and are champions at long-distance running. An Asian horse called the onager can run at about 28 miles per hour. It can continue to run for hours without tiring.

he fastest-
unning mammal
n earth is the cheetah.
can capture its prey by
unning as fast as *70 miles per
our*—faster than the speed limit
n most freeways!

The red fox has only average running speed—about 26 miles per hour. But its agility and endurance as a runner allow it to wear down its prey and pounce on it.

With no legs at all, the mamba snake can crawl on its belly at a speed of 12 miles per hour, either in pursuit of prey or to escape danger. It is the fastest land snake in the world.

Each animal's physical structure makes it a champion for its life-style and in its environment. That's because, in nature, abilities and structure are tailored to needs. Cheetahs use lightning fast bursts of speed to overtake their prey quickly. Wild horses have great endurance so they can outlast their predators in a race for survival.

A tortoise has no need for speed. It doesn't need to chase its food, because it eats plants. It doesn't need to run away, because it carries its protective shell with it. But not all tortoises are alike. They have different structural adaptations that suit them to their environments.

Tortoises with domed shells eat plants that are low growing. Some giant tortoises have *saddle-backed* shells that rise high in the front to let the tortoise stretch its long neck upward. These tortoises live on islands where the cactus they eat grows tall, and they must stretch to reach it.

A long stride helps animals run fast. The secret to a cheetah's long stride is its flexible spine. As its spine bends upward, the cheetah's hind legs actually reach *ahead* of its front legs. To see how this works, bend a pipe cleaner back and forth. You can bend the ends close together and then extend them again because the pipe cleaner is flexible, like the cheetah's spine.

As the cheetah's spine straightens, its legs extend far out in front and in back of its body. With each stride, this graceful cat covers a lot of ground. Even though it has much shorter legs than an onager, its stride is actually longer.

The way a snake moves, by pressing its ribs against the ground, is not very fast. Once its prey starts to run away, even the fastest snake cannot catch up with it. But when a snake takes an animal by surprise, it can lunge forward to strike quicker than the eye can see.

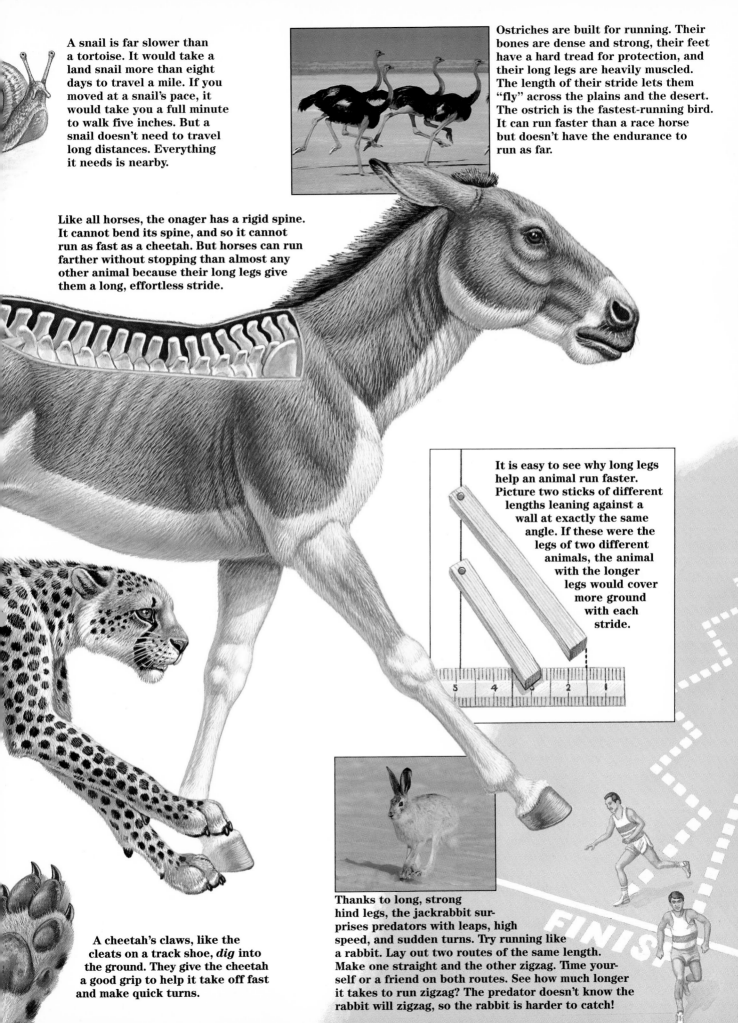

A snail is far slower than a tortoise. It would take a land snail more than eight days to travel a mile. If you moved at a snail's pace, it would take you a full minute to walk five inches. But a snail doesn't need to travel long distances. Everything it needs is nearby.

Ostriches are built for running. Their bones are dense and strong, their feet have a hard tread for protection, and their long legs are heavily muscled. The length of their stride lets them "fly" across the plains and the desert. The ostrich is the fastest-running bird. It can run faster than a race horse but doesn't have the endurance to run as far.

Like all horses, the onager has a rigid spine. It cannot bend its spine, and so it cannot run as fast as a cheetah. But horses can run farther without stopping than almost any other animal because their long legs give them a long, effortless stride.

It is easy to see why long legs help an animal run faster. Picture two sticks of different lengths leaning against a wall at exactly the same angle. If these were the legs of two different animals, the animal with the longer legs would cover more ground with each stride.

A cheetah's claws, like the cleats on a track shoe, *dig* into the ground. They give the cheetah a good grip to help it take off fast and make quick turns.

Thanks to long, strong hind legs, the jackrabbit surprises predators with leaps, high speed, and sudden turns. Try running like a rabbit. Lay out two routes of the same length. Make one straight and the other zigzag. Time yourself or a friend on both routes. See how much longer it takes to run zigzag? The predator doesn't know the rabbit will zigzag, so the rabbit is harder to catch!

FINISH

9

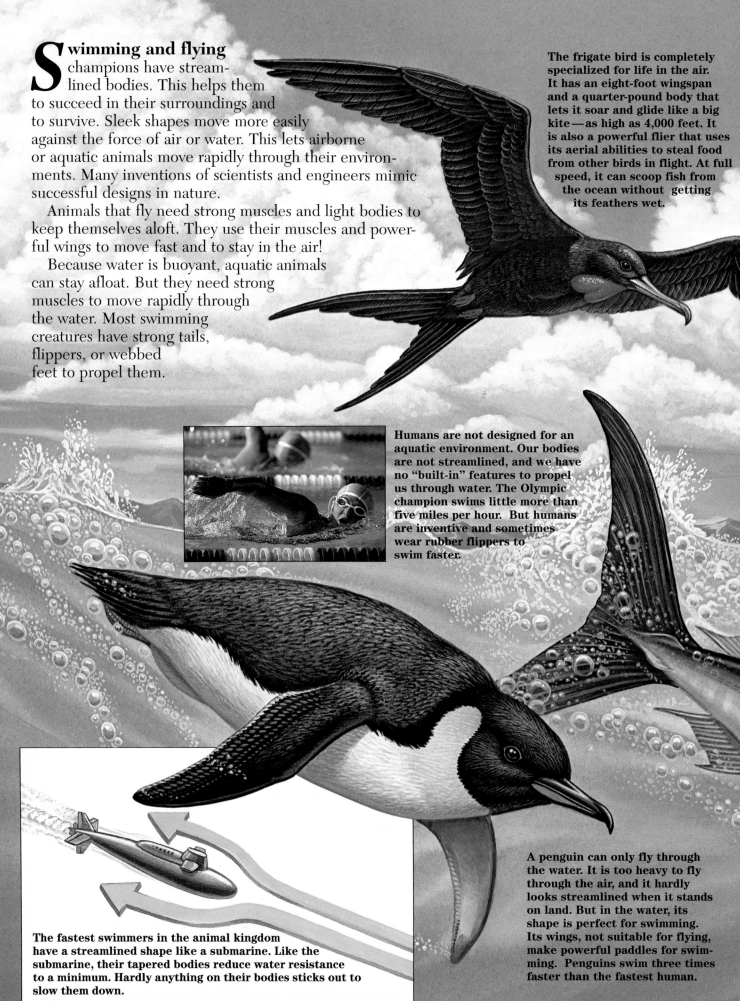

S wimming and flying champions have stream-lined bodies. This helps them to succeed in their surroundings and to survive. Sleek shapes move more easily against the force of air or water. This lets airborne or aquatic animals move rapidly through their environ-ments. Many inventions of scientists and engineers mimic successful designs in nature.

Animals that fly need strong muscles and light bodies to keep themselves aloft. They use their muscles and power-ful wings to move fast and to stay in the air!

Because water is buoyant, aquatic animals can stay afloat. But they need strong muscles to move rapidly through the water. Most swimming creatures have strong tails, flippers, or webbed feet to propel them.

The frigate bird is completely specialized for life in the air. It has an eight-foot wingspan and a quarter-pound body that lets it soar and glide like a big kite—as high as 4,000 feet. It is also a powerful flier that uses its aerial abilities to steal food from other birds in flight. At full speed, it can scoop fish from the ocean without getting its feathers wet.

Humans are not designed for an aquatic environment. Our bodies are not streamlined, and we have no "built-in" features to propel us through water. The Olympic champion swims little more than five miles per hour. But humans are inventive and sometimes wear rubber flippers to swim faster.

The fastest swimmers in the animal kingdom have a streamlined shape like a submarine. Like the submarine, their tapered bodies reduce water resistance to a minimum. Hardly anything on their bodies sticks out to slow them down.

A penguin can only fly through the water. It is too heavy to fly through the air, and it hardly looks streamlined when it stands on land. But in the water, its shape is perfect for swimming. Its wings, not suitable for flying, make powerful paddles for swim-ming. Penguins swim three times faster than the fastest human.

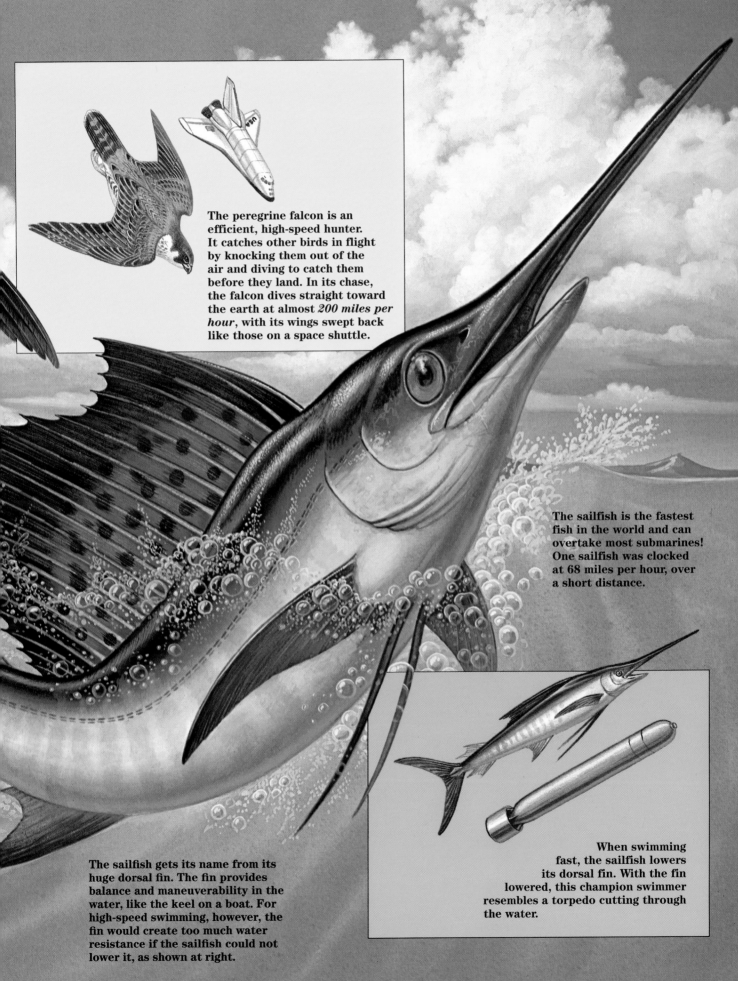

The peregrine falcon is an efficient, high-speed hunter. It catches other birds in flight by knocking them out of the air and diving to catch them before they land. In its chase, the falcon dives straight toward the earth at almost *200 miles per hour*, with its wings swept back like those on a space shuttle.

The sailfish is the fastest fish in the world and can overtake most submarines! One sailfish was clocked at 68 miles per hour, over a short distance.

The sailfish gets its name from its huge dorsal fin. The fin provides balance and maneuverability in the water, like the keel on a boat. For high-speed swimming, however, the fin would create too much water resistance if the sailfish could not lower it, as shown at right.

When swimming fast, the sailfish lowers its dorsal fin. With the fin lowered, this champion swimmer resembles a torpedo cutting through the water.

Distance champions in the animal world fly higher, dive deeper, and travel farther than you can imagine. Their search for food, their migrations to far-off wintering grounds, and their return to breeding grounds require remarkable endurance. These animal champions have bodies specially equipped to perform the feats that help them survive. It is often the urge to reproduce and replenish their species that triggers their spectacular achievements.

One of the highest-flying birds in the world is the bar-headed goose of Asia. These geese breed near lakes high in the mountains of central Asia, and each year they migrate south to winter in India. To reach their wintering grounds, they must fly over the Himalayas—the world's highest mountain range. Bar-headed geese have been seen flying at almost 28,000 feet during their migration.

Some seemingly delicate butterflies have great endurance. They fly south in winter to seek warmer climates, and in the spring they fly north to lay their eggs. Their journeys often take them over high mountain ranges, and wind currents can carry them to the level of high-flying airplanes. The migratory urge is important to their life cycle and compels them to return to their original breeding grounds each year.

Whales are the deep-sea diving champions among mammals. Like humans and other mammals, whales cannot breathe underwater. But they can store great amounts of oxygen in their muscles. Before diving, the gigantic sperm whale can store enough oxygen to hold its breath for two hours. This allows it to dive nearly two miles deep to catch a favorite meal—about 400 pounds of squid!

Caribou spend much of their lives on the march. In summer, they migrate to calving grounds in the far north of their Arctic habitat. In fall, they migrate south to winter in Arctic woodlands. Their bodies are adapted to life in the dark cold of long northern nights. They find plants to eat beneath the snow, but must continue to move in order to find enough food for herds that number in the thousands. The caribou's splayed feet are suited to walking in the snow and swamps of the tundra.

Chinook salmon are long-distance swimming champions. After spending several years at sea, the adult salmon travel as far as 2,500 miles or more to return to the freshwater spawning grounds where they hatched. The reproductive urge drives them, and their sense of smell leads them up rivers left years before. The salmon swim against strong currents and leap 10-foot waterfalls to get "home." After the eggs of a new generation are deposited, fertilized, and covered for protection, the adult salmon die, exhausted by the journey.

The monarch butterfly migrates about 2,000 miles one way. Because it often rides the wind and saves energy, it can travel about 600 miles on a single meal of nectar.

The greatest traveler of all is the Arctic tern. It spends its summers in the northern Arctic, where it nests in up to 24 hours of daylight. Then it migrates south for a second "summer" in the Antarctic. Its annual round trip between the North Pole and the South Pole takes it about 20,000 miles. In a lifetime of 20 or 30 years, an Arctic tern may log as many as one-half million miles!

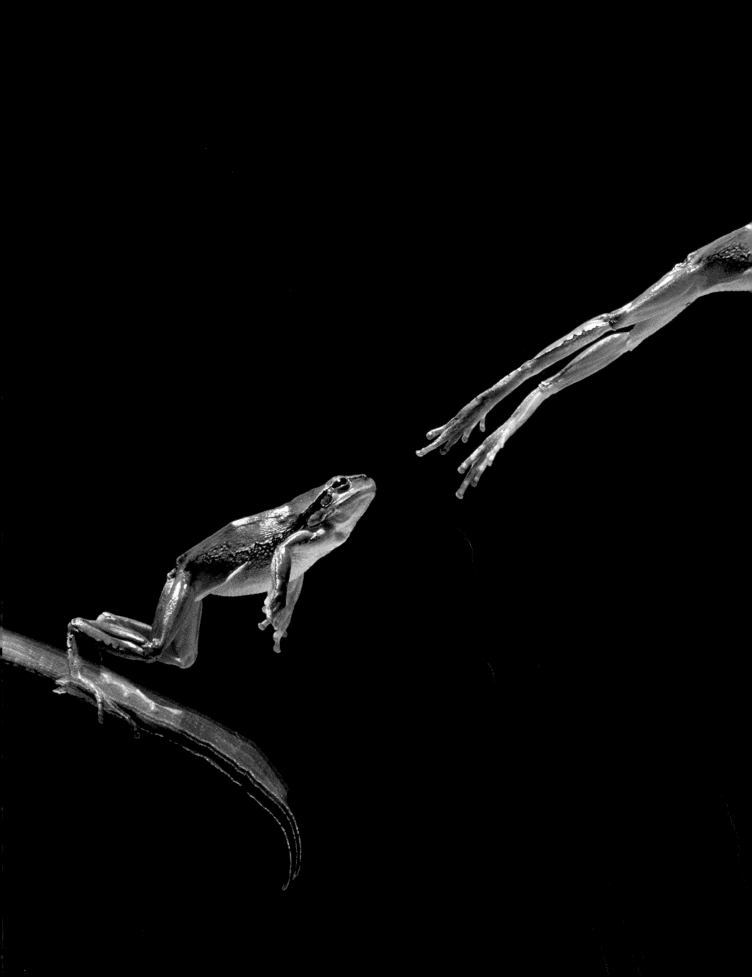

Tree frogs are built to jump. Their long back legs give
them a good send-off, and their fingers are equipped with
adhesive pads that can grab a branch or reed securely. A
tree frog launches itself at a target with such accuracy
that it can scoop up and swallow an insect while landing.
This two-inch-long European tree frog can leap three feet
or more.

Jumping champions have strong legs that work like springs. Their back legs do the work and are often longer than their front legs. Sometimes they also have large back feet to aid push-off and landing.

Jumping animals don't just jump for joy. They jump because their lives depend on it. Some jump to capture prey, others leap to elude predators. By jumping, those that live in arid regions, where food is sparse, can cover great distances to forage.

It's not easy to choose a champion among champions, because they all jump in manners appropriate to their needs and their environments. The kangaroo may spring the farthest, but the flea, for its size, wins the prize!

If you could jump as well as a flea, you could leap a 50-story building in a single bound.

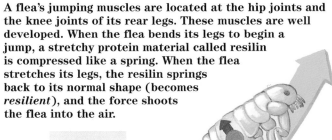

A flea's jumping muscles are located at the hip joints and the knee joints of its rear legs. These muscles are well developed. When the flea bends its legs to begin a jump, a stretchy protein material called resilin is compressed like a spring. When the flea stretches its legs, the resilin springs back to its normal shape (becomes *resilient*), and the force shoots the flea into the air.

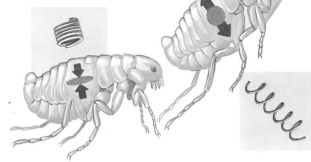

The jumping spider pounces on its prey and, nine times out of ten, lands right on target. Adhesive hairs on its feet keep it from slipping, and the placement of its eight eyes—four in a row at the front of its head—helps it to be accurate. Unlike many champion jumpers, the jumping spider's *front* legs are the longest. Its short back legs make the leap, and the long front legs hold down the prey.

If all the animals shown at right were entered in a jumping contest, it would be hard to pick the winner. But the elephant would be a sure loser. With its heavy body and legs that can barely bend, it can't jump at all. And doesn't need to!

ANIMAL OLYMPICS

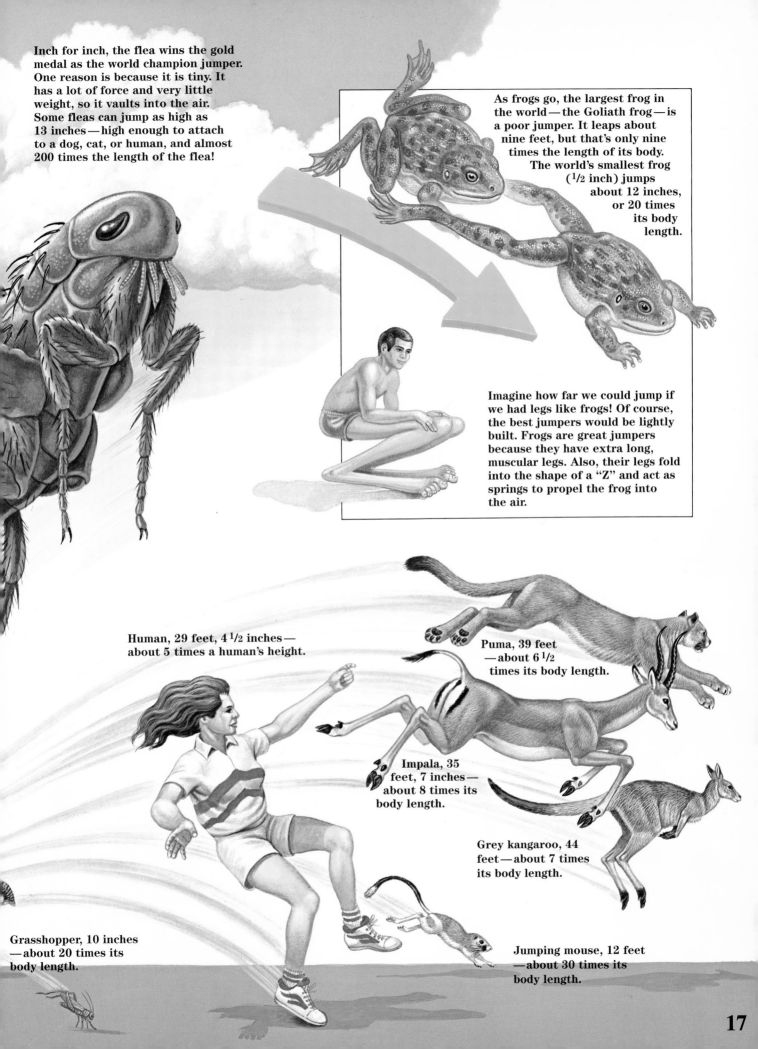

Inch for inch, the flea wins the gold medal as the world champion jumper. One reason is because it is tiny. It has a lot of force and very little weight, so it vaults into the air. Some fleas can jump as high as 13 inches—high enough to attach to a dog, cat, or human, and almost 200 times the length of the flea!

As frogs go, the largest frog in the world—the Goliath frog—is a poor jumper. It leaps about nine feet, but that's only nine times the length of its body. The world's smallest frog (¹/₂ inch) jumps about 12 inches, or 20 times its body length.

Imagine how far we could jump if we had legs like frogs! Of course, the best jumpers would be lightly built. Frogs are great jumpers because they have extra long, muscular legs. Also, their legs fold into the shape of a "Z" and act as springs to propel the frog into the air.

Human, 29 feet, 4 ¹/₂ inches— about 5 times a human's height.

Puma, 39 feet —about 6 ¹/₂ times its body length.

Impala, 35 feet, 7 inches— about 8 times its body length.

Grey kangaroo, 44 feet—about 7 times its body length.

Grasshopper, 10 inches —about 20 times its body length.

Jumping mouse, 12 feet —about 30 times its body length.

Basilisks are swimming, diving, and *running* champions. They run on land, and they run on water! A broad surface on their back feet keeps them from sinking. They run so fast (about 7 1/2 miles per hour) that their feet barely touch the water. This ability aids their survival, because a runner can outdistance a swimmer.

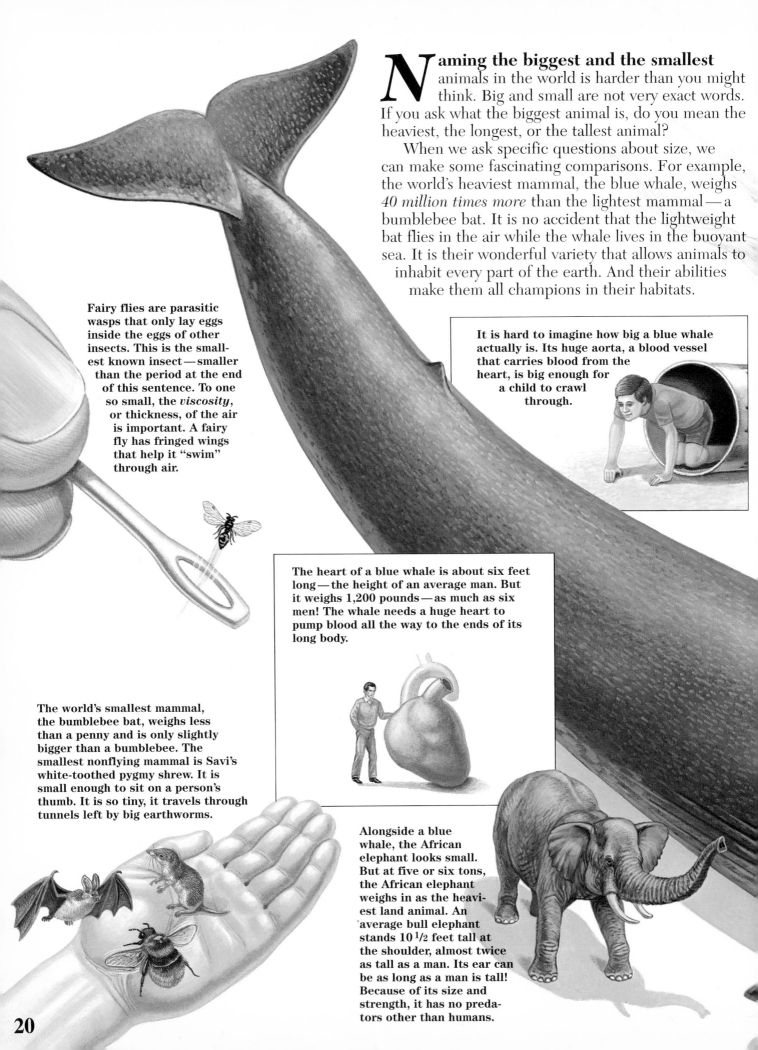

Naming the biggest and the smallest animals in the world is harder than you might think. Big and small are not very exact words. If you ask what the biggest animal is, do you mean the heaviest, the longest, or the tallest animal?

When we ask specific questions about size, we can make some fascinating comparisons. For example, the world's heaviest mammal, the blue whale, weighs *40 million times more* than the lightest mammal—a bumblebee bat. It is no accident that the lightweight bat flies in the air while the whale lives in the buoyant sea. It is their wonderful variety that allows animals to inhabit every part of the earth. And their abilities make them all champions in their habitats.

Fairy flies are parasitic wasps that only lay eggs inside the eggs of other insects. This is the smallest known insect—smaller than the period at the end of this sentence. To one so small, the *viscosity*, or thickness, of the air is important. A fairy fly has fringed wings that help it "swim" through air.

It is hard to imagine how big a blue whale actually is. Its huge aorta, a blood vessel that carries blood from the heart, is big enough for a child to crawl through.

The heart of a blue whale is about six feet long—the height of an average man. But it weighs 1,200 pounds—as much as six men! The whale needs a huge heart to pump blood all the way to the ends of its long body.

The world's smallest mammal, the bumblebee bat, weighs less than a penny and is only slightly bigger than a bumblebee. The smallest nonflying mammal is Savi's white-toothed pygmy shrew. It is small enough to sit on a person's thumb. It is so tiny, it travels through tunnels left by big earthworms.

Alongside a blue whale, the African elephant looks small. But at five or six tons, the African elephant weighs in as the heaviest land animal. An average bull elephant stands 10 1/2 feet tall at the shoulder, almost twice as tall as a man. Its ear can be as long as a man is tall! Because of its size and strength, it has no predators other than humans.

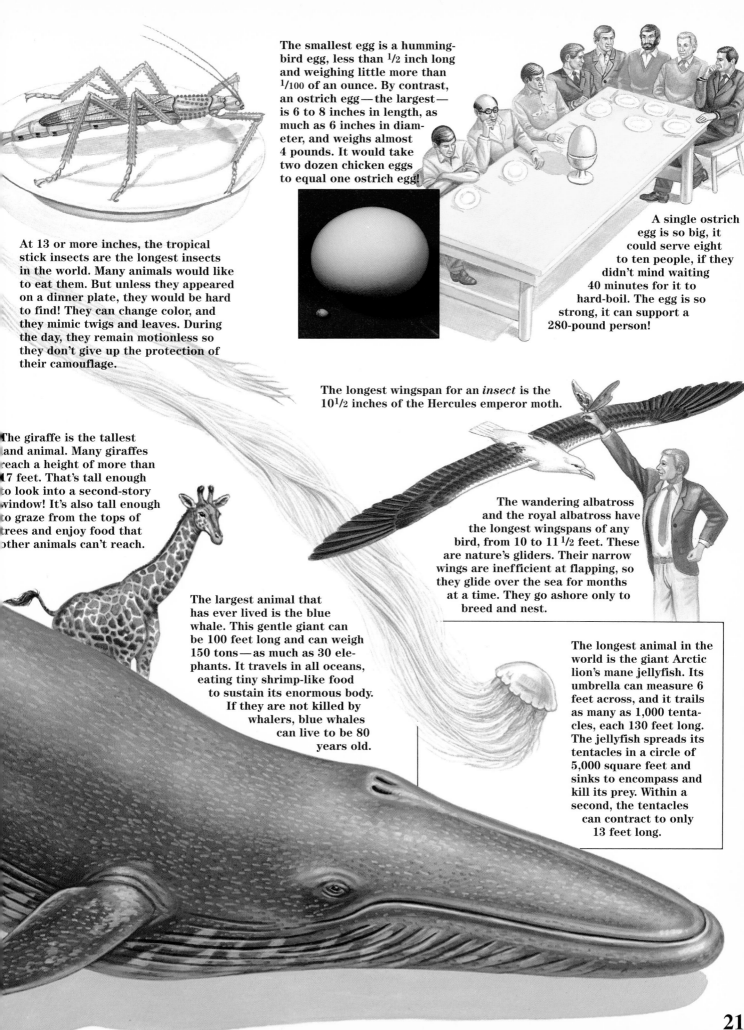

At 13 or more inches, the tropical stick insects are the longest insects in the world. Many animals would like to eat them. But unless they appeared on a dinner plate, they would be hard to find! They can change color, and they mimic twigs and leaves. During the day, they remain motionless so they don't give up the protection of their camouflage.

The smallest egg is a hummingbird egg, less than $1/2$ inch long and weighing little more than $1/100$ of an ounce. By contrast, an ostrich egg—the largest—is 6 to 8 inches in length, as much as 6 inches in diameter, and weighs almost 4 pounds. It would take two dozen chicken eggs to equal one ostrich egg!

A single ostrich egg is so big, it could serve eight to ten people, if they didn't mind waiting 40 minutes for it to hard-boil. The egg is so strong, it can support a 280-pound person!

The giraffe is the tallest land animal. Many giraffes reach a height of more than 17 feet. That's tall enough to look into a second-story window! It's also tall enough to graze from the tops of trees and enjoy food that other animals can't reach.

The longest wingspan for an *insect* is the $10 1/2$ inches of the Hercules emperor moth.

The wandering albatross and the royal albatross have the longest wingspans of any bird, from 10 to $11 1/2$ feet. These are nature's gliders. Their narrow wings are inefficient at flapping, so they glide over the sea for months at a time. They go ashore only to breed and nest.

The largest animal that has ever lived is the blue whale. This gentle giant can be 100 feet long and can weigh 150 tons—as much as 30 elephants. It travels in all oceans, eating tiny shrimp-like food to sustain its enormous body. If they are not killed by whalers, blue whales can live to be 80 years old.

The longest animal in the world is the giant Arctic lion's mane jellyfish. Its umbrella can measure 6 feet across, and it trails as many as 1,000 tentacles, each 130 feet long. The jellyfish spreads its tentacles in a circle of 5,000 square feet and sinks to encompass and kill its prey. Within a second, the tentacles can contract to only 13 feet long.

21

The strongest animals are not always the biggest. True, the largest animals in the world, whales and elephants, can lift and pull astonishing weights. But does that make them the strongest animals? For its size, the world's strongest animal is probably the ant. It can lift and carry objects many times its own size.

In nature, animals do what is necessary for their survival. In the course of their development over millions of years, they have adapted to their environments and acquired the strengths necessary to make them champions in their own realms.

An insect does not have bones inside its body. Instead it has an *exoskeleton*, an external skeleton that wraps around the *outside* of its body. In relation to an animal's size, the exoskeletal covering of an insect is stronger than the solid *endoskeleton* of a human. Its exoskeleton allows an insect to carry heavy weights.

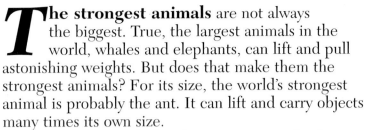

SEE FOR YOURSELF

See for yourself how a "hollow" external skeleton can be stronger than solid bone. Take two identical pieces of paper. Roll one into a solid tube and the other into a hollow tube. Try to bend both tubes, and you will see that the hollow tube is harder to bend.

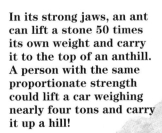

In its strong jaws, an ant can lift a stone 50 times its own weight and carry it to the top of an anthill. A person with the same proportionate strength could lift a car weighing nearly four tons and carry it up a hill!

Because of its massive size, the blue whale is probably the most powerful creature on earth. A story is told about a blue whale that was once harpooned by fishermen aboard a 90-foot motor boat. For 7 hours, the harpooned whale tugged the boat across 50 miles of ocean. The whole time, the boat was pulling against the whale with its engines running full speed *in reverse!*

No other land animal can lift as much *total* weight as the Asian elephant. It can lift a ton of logs with its trunk. And it can *drag* a 10-ton bundle of logs, which is twice its own weight.

Some *human* champions can lift more than three times their body weight. But a chimpanzee can lift *six times its weight.* Chimpanzees have stronger upper bodies than humans. The ape with the greatest upper body strength is the orangutan. It is truly arboreal, swinging from tree to tree and supporting its body weight with its arms.

For animals to survive on earth, there is no set requirement for success. It is not necessarily important to be the fastest, the strongest, the most spectacular, to have the greatest endurance, or to set the most records. The real champions in the life process are those who have managed to adapt to their environments over many millions of years and to survive the pressures that surround them. It has taken a long time to produce these champions. When their environments are changed rapidly, these long-term champions cannot adjust fast enough to survive the change.

Index